ON THE MOVE...

MOVING A ROCKET,
A SUB,
and LONDON BRIDGE

By David Paige

 CHILDRENS PRESS, CHICAGO

London Bridge is very busy in this print from about 1872.

Library of Congress Cataloging in Publication Data

Moving a rocket, a sub, and London Bridge.

(On the move)
SUMMARY: Examines the special equipment and
procedures used to move the London Bridge, a WWII
German submarine, and the Saturn rocket with its Apollo
spacecraft.
1. Moving of buildings, bridges, etc.—Juvenile
literature. 2. London Bridge—Juvenile literature.
3. Project Saturn—Juvenile literature. 4. U-505
(Submarine)—Juvenile literature. [1. Moving of
buildings, bridges, etc. 2. London Bridge.
3. Project Saturn. 4. U-505 (Submarine)] I. Title.
TH149.W48   629.04'9   80-22125
ISBN 0-516-03890-7

Photographs courtesy of Historical Pictures Service,
Inc., Chicago, 2, 4; Wide World Photos, 9, 10, 14, 33;
Lake Havasu City Chamber of Commerce, 13;
Museum of Science and Industry, Chicago, 16, 24, 26,
28, 29; United Press International, 21, 22; NASA, 30,
34, 35, 36, 37, 41, 42.
Front cover; Saturn V, NASA
Back cover; The U-505, Museum of Science and
Industry, Chicago

MOVING THE LONDON BRIDGE
TO ARIZONA

"London Bridge is falling down." The song and rhyme have said this for hundreds of years. But none of them ever really fell down. They were just taken down when it was thought they were unsafe.

There has, in fact, been a "London Bridge" since about 50 A.D. It is over the River Thames. The Romans, it is thought, built a wooden bridge about that time. It was in almost the same spot as the London Bridge of today. This is just west of the Tower of London and the Tower Bridge.

Above: Old London Bridge as it looked in 1760

Below: Traffic on Sir John's bridge in about 1890

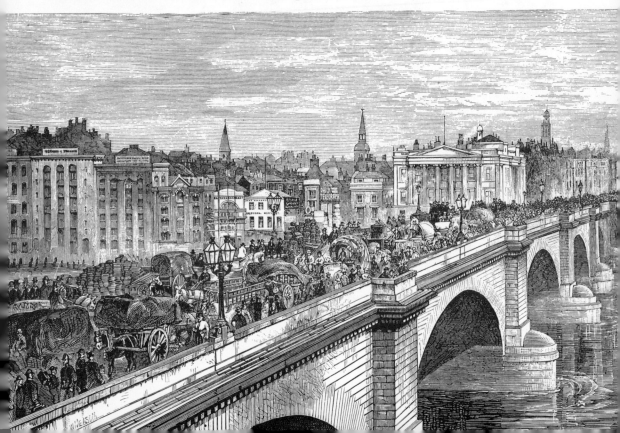

By the year 1209, the Roman bridge had been replaced. The new London Bridge was made of stone. It lasted for more than six hundred years. Then, in 1831, a Scottish <u>engineer</u> named Sir John Rennie built an even newer London Bridge. It had been planned by his father. This bridge served Londoners until 1967.

But this very heavy bridge had its problems. It had been sinking into the Thames River bed. It sank about one inch every eight years. The sinking made some bad cracks in the bridge. It too would have to be removed.

It was quite a job. Sir John's bridge was very large. It was made of hard rock called <u>granite.</u> It was 1,005 feet long. And the granite weighed about 130,000 tons. Four lanes of traffic crossed at once. The bridge also had five arches. Its center span was 152 feet long.

Underlined words are defined in the glossary in the back of the book.

In London the government didn't want
to destroy the bridge. They called it an
"outstanding example of 19th century
skill in <u>masonry design</u> and construction."
So they offered it for sale. But, they said,
"the bridge [must] be <u>preserved</u> and
reassembled into a new bridge of similar
shape and size."

There were not many real offers. But
there was one. It came from the
McCullouch Corporation of California.
They offered about $2.5 million for the
bridge. They said they would transport it
to Lake Havasu City. This is a resort and
retirement spot in Arizona. It is on the
banks of the Colorado River.

The offer was accepted. It was announced that the bridge was going to be moved to the famous American West. A London newspaper ran the headline:

LONDON BRIDGE SOLD TO APACHES

It cost about another $3 million to move London Bridge to Arizona and rebuild it there. All of the bridge was not moved. Only the granite <u>facing</u>, or outside, was taken. This was about 10,000 tons of granite. The <u>core</u>, or center, of the bridge was destroyed. London Bridge was rebuilt around a new core. A new bridge would have cost less. But it would not bring the visitors that London Bridge would.

The job of taking London Bridge down began in 1967. Meanwhile, in London, a new bridge was being built next to it. That was so Londoners would not be without their own London Bridge.

Taking Sir John's bridge down was well-planned. It was taken apart in blocks. The blocks were different sizes. They weighed from a half-ton to five tons each.

A numbering system was made for the blocks. Then, large drawings of the bridge were made. Each block or section of the bridge was given a number. The drawings looked like large "paint-by-number" drawings. The numbers showed where each granite block belonged. The bridge could be rebuilt just as it had stood before.

Putting the bridge in place in Lake Havasu City

By September 1971, most of the granite facing was up.

Numbers were painted on each block of stone on the bridge. This was done before that block was removed. The painted number was then covered with a <u>lacquer.</u> This helped protect it from the weather. It also protected it when it rubbed against other blocks.

Each block of granite was then pried loose from the bridge—one at a time. A machine called an <u>hydraulic excavator</u> was used. It had a <u>pneumatic "breaker"</u> that looked like a giant toothpick. The breaker loosened the block of stone. Then the machine, acting as a crane, lifted the block of stone away. Some blocks could not be reached by the <u>excavator.</u> They were loosened by stoneworkers using pneumatic drills. Then each of these blocks was lifted away by a <u>crane.</u>

A few of the blocks were damaged. Only about three out of every 100 broke. Most were fixed with an <u>epoxy resin.</u> In a few cases the blocks had to be replaced. Then other blocks from the core of the bridge were used.

The giant stone blocks were removed. They were packed on a truck. They were brought to a dock on the Thames River. Here the blocks were loaded on cargo ships. The ships then hauled them across the Atlantic Ocean. They passed through the Panama Canal. They went up the Pacific Coast to the port at Long Beach, California. There, London Bridge, in pieces, entered the United States free of <u>duty.</u> The stones were called parts of "a large <u>antique.</u>"

The granite blocks were then moved by truck. They traveled 300 miles inland to Lake Havasu City. They were lined up there like building blocks.

The rebuilt London Bridge

In Lake Havasu City, a narrow <u>channel</u> was dug. Water from the Colorado River was fed into it. This man-made waterway was named Little Thames River. Over it, the London Bridge was rebuilt. A new core was built. About 10,000 tons of the granite facing from the first London Bridge was put up.

A large ceremony was planned at Lake
Havasu City. This was for the laying of the
first granite block. The Lord Mayor of
London came from England. Many
important Americans came. The first
block was carefully moved into place.
School children sang the old rhyme.
They just changed the words a little:
"London Bridge is going up . . ."

GETTING THE U-505 TO CHICAGO

In September 1954, some motorists saw a strange traffic sign:

CAUTION
Submarine Crossing

This was on a road in Chicago that runs along the shore of Lake Michigan.

It was no joke. The U-505, a German U-boat (submarine) was about to be moved from the lake and across the road. It would be placed next to the city's Museum of Science and Industry. There it would stand as a war <u>memorial</u>. It would also be an <u>exhibit</u> open to the public.

The U-505, in 1954, on the beach in Chicago

How the U-505 came a thousand miles inland in the United States is a wonder.

Germany built 1,162 U-boats during World War II. They roamed the Atlantic Ocean. They were alone or in groups called "wolf packs." They were in search of Allied ships to sink.

The U-505 was launched in 1941. It came from the German port of Hamburg. First, it went on practice maneuvers in the Baltic Sea. The sub was tested. Its crew trained for war. Its first real "war" voyage came in the beginning of 1942. During the next two and a half years, its torpedoes sank at least seven enemy freighters and tankers. They sent almost 50,000 tons of cargo to the bottom of the ocean. The sub also escaped some dangerous meetings with American warplanes and Allied warships.

But in June 1944, the U-505's luck ran out. The sub was in the Atlantic Ocean. It was south of the Canary Islands. It was about 150 miles off Africa's Gold Coast. Also in the same area was a U.S. Navy task group. This group had an aircraft carrier and five destroyers. Their mission was to hunt down and destroy submarines.

Captain Daniel V. Gallery was the commander of the U.S. task group. Sinking subs was his business. But he also knew it would be great to *capture* one, somehow—probably by boarding it.

An enemy sub had never been captured in that way before. In fact, the Navy had not captured a <u>foreign</u> warship of any kind by boarding since 1815. But maybe it could be done. Captain Gallery trained the crews of his six ships. The crews learned to carry out a capture operation.

The chance to put that training to a real test came on June 4, 1944. That day one of Captain Gallery's destroyers made sonar contact with the U-505 off the coast of Africa. The destroyer attacked with explosive <u>depth charges.</u> Other ships moved in to cut off escape. Planes from the aircraft carrier circled overhead. They were ready to <u>zero in.</u> Their machine guns were ready for when the U-boat <u>surfaced.</u>

The U-505 had no chance. It took a direct hit from one of the depth charges. The damage was great. The sub commander was forced to bring his boat to the surface. He wanted to save his crew. The sub, he knew, was about to sink. So he <u>abandoned</u> the U-505.

But to his surprise, there was a boarding party from the U.S. task group in a small boat. They got to the damaged sub before it went down. The sea was rough. Huge waves washed over the deck of the sinking sub. But the men were able to go below. They found German <u>documents</u>, log books, and the important <u>code books.</u> Then one of the destroyers pulled alongside. Its pumps were used to get the water out of the U-505. The boarding party hooked up a <u>tow line</u> between the sub and the aircraft carrier. This kept the U-boat afloat. The U-505 had been captured.

The U-505 is boarded.

The escort carrier *USS Guadalcanal* is in the background.

Other ships of the task group collected the crew of the U-505 from the ocean waters. They took them aboard as prisoners of war. A U.S. Navy tugboat was called to tow the U-505. It went 1,700 miles back across the Atlantic Ocean. It stopped at an Allied port on the island of Bermuda.

The whole action was a secret. The prisoners had no way to get word back to Germany. The 3,000 American sailors of the task group were sworn to <u>secrecy</u>. The Germans thought the U-505 had been lost in battle. They thought it rested somewhere on the floor of the Atlantic Ocean. They did not know that their enemies were studying it. They did not know the Americans had the German naval code book. It was one of the great <u>feats</u> of World War II.

When the war was over, the U-505 was brought to the submarine base at Portsmouth, New Hampshire. It stayed there until 1954. The U.S. Navy felt it no longer had any use for the sub. They decided the U-505 would be <u>scrapped.</u> They would save anything of value. They would get rid of the rest as junk. Certain people in Chicago, Illinois, heard of this. They decided to do something about it.

The U-505 arrives in Chicago.

First, they raised $250,000. This would pay the cost of bringing the U-505 to Chicago. Next, an Act of Congress gave them legal title to the vessel. Then, all they had to do was move the sub to Chicago.

The first 3,000 miles were easy. It was the last 800 feet that were a problem. The U-505 was hitched to a tugboat. The tugboat towed it from Portsmouth harbor. It went down through Lakes Ontario and Erie. It went up through Lake Huron and down Lake Michigan to Chicago. This trip took a month.

Then came the hard part. That was getting the sub up out of the water and across the road. On land it needed to be settled into its _berth_ next to the museum. The sub weighed 1,000 tons. It was 252 feet long.

A plan was drawn up. It called for placing the U-505 in a _floating dry dock._ This was the shape of a huge shoe box. Inside this giant box, the sub was put on steel rollers and rails. This would help move it later. _Support beams_ from the sides of the dry dock held the sub in place.

At the same time, a 50-foot _pier_ was built out into the lake. This was from the spot on the beach where the sub would be unloaded. A channel also had to be dug out from the end of the pier. The channel was 325 feet long. It was nine feet below the surface of the water. This stopped the floating dry dock from running _aground._

The dry dock was moved into place at the pier. The U-boat was slowly and carefully rolled out of it onto the pier. A strong winch with four cables pulled the U-505 from the dry dock. As the sub's weight was moving off the dry dock, an equal weight of water had to be pumped into special tanks in the dry dock. This kept the sub steady and in place. This meant that as each four feet of sub moved onto the pier, 27 tons of water had to be poured into the dry dock's tanks.

On shore, the U-505 had to be raised four feet, four inches to pass over the road. Then it was on the museum ground. The sub and its carriage of rollers and rails was raised by using 42 mechanical jacks.

At seven o'clock on the night of
September 3, 1954, all traffic was stopped
on the road. The sub began its move
across—rear end first. It would not be on
the other side of the road until 4:15 the
next morning. This was more than nine
hours later.

The U-505 was moved another 100
yards or so. Then it reached the spot where
it was to stay, next to the museum. Here
it was hung over three concrete cradles.
Each cradle would support a third of the

sub's weight. The U-505 was slowly
lowered. Concrete arms and supports
were later added to hold the sub in place.

Since then, millions of people have
walked through the U-505's cabins,
compartments, and engine rooms. They
have looked into its conning tower. They
have gazed at its periscope and torpedo
tubes. They have seen all the controls and
equipment that are part of a sub.
Everything is just as it was when the U-505
moved silently beneath the water in
search of ships to attack.

MOVING *SATURN V* INTO SPACE

The *Saturn V* rocket is a real mover itself. It moved <u>astronauts</u> and their *Apollo* spacecrafts into outer space.

The National Aeronautics and Space Administration, called NASA, is in charge of rocket launchings. Usually all work is done right at the <u>launch pad</u>. But *Saturn V* was the largest rocket ever built. It was built in three separate stages.

The three stages were built in different places. Then they had to be moved to Cape Canaveral, Florida. Here the stages were checked out. They were <u>assembled.</u> Then they were moved to the launch pad.

Each stage of the rocket was very large. The total length of the rocket was about 365 feet. That is longer than a football field. When stood up for launch, it was about the height of a 35-story building.

Two of the stages of *Saturn V* were shipped from California. They were moved on ocean-going <u>barges.</u> They were carried down the Pacific Coast to the Panama Canal. They went through the Caribbean Sea. They followed the Atlantic Ocean to Cape Canaveral and unloaded.

The smallest stage of the rocket was shipped on a plane. It was a special super-large transport plane called the "Guppy."

At Cape Canaveral, NASA built a special launch area for the *Saturn V*. It was called "Launch Complex 39." It also had one of the largest <u>land vehicles</u> ever made. Launch Complex 39 had six parts. This doesn't count the launch pad itself. Each part was important in getting *Saturn V* to its launch pad.

Saturn V on its barge

First, there was the Vehicle Assembly
Building. NASA called this VAB. It was
the largest <u>scientific</u> building in the
world. The VAB was built only to test and
assemble the *Saturn V*. The building is
716 feet long. It is 518 feet wide and 525
feet high. It covers 343,500 square feet of
floor space. The VAB has four doors. Each
door is 456 feet tall.

Vehicle Assembly Building

The Launch Control Center is another part of the area. It is a four-story building. It sits next to the VAB. It is where parts of *Saturn V* were tested.

The <u>Mobile Launcher</u> was really the rocket's platform. It was also the tower that held the *Saturn V*. It was brought into the VAB. There the fully assembled *Saturn V* was joined with it.

Mobile Launcher

The Mobile Launcher had a two-story base. Its tower extended 398 feet above the launch platform. Arms from the tower attached to the *Saturn V*. The entire Mobile Launcher was 445 feet high. Along with the *Saturn V* it weighed about 12 million pounds. The base on which the *Saturn V* sat covered about a half acre. The tower also held an elevator. The elevator took the astronauts up to the *Apollo* spacecraft. They entered the <u>space capsule</u> through one of the tower arms.

Transporter

The *Saturn V* was assembled. It was
tested. It was <u>attached</u> to the Mobile
Launcher. Then it had to be moved from
the VAB to the launch pad. This was about
3 1/2 miles. A very special mover had to
be built. A very powerful trucklike
vehicle was built. It was called the
Marion 8-Caterpillar Crawler. It was the
biggest vehicle ever <u>constructed.</u> NASA
calls this vehicle the Transporter. But some
Transporter! It weighed six million
pounds. It was 131 feet long. It was 114 feet
wide. Its windshield wipers were 3 1/2
feet tall. The largest wipers ever made.

The Transporter moved on four
<u>double-tracked crawlers.</u> Each crawler was
10 feet high and 40 feet long. Two mighty
diesel engines, 2,750 horsepower each,
provided the power. (A car's <u>horsepower</u>
ranges from 50 to 300.) This vehicle could
only move its load at one mile per hour.
In fact, it took about six hours to move
Saturn V to its launch pad. The
Transporter could not keep its top speed
all during the 3 1/2 mile trip.

The Transporter carried 18 million
pounds. So it could not go over a normal
road. A special "Crawlerway" was built. It
was a road, but it was 131 feet wide. It
was about the size of an eight-lane
highway. It even had a <u>median strip.</u> The
Crawlerway was built in layers. It was

about seven feet deep. The first 2 1/2 feet
were a very <u>compacted hydraulic fill</u>. That
means it was hardened with water. The
next layer was three feet of crushed rock.
Then another layer was spread. This was
about a foot thick. A six-inch covering of
river rock was then added. Finally the
whole roadway was sealed with asphalt.

The *Saturn V* and its Mobile Launcher
were moved over the Crawlerway. They
reached the launch pad. They were raised
into position for blast-off. But the
operation was still not complete.

About 7,000 feet from the launch pad
was a towerlike structure. It was the
Mobile Service Structure. It was 402 feet
tall. It weighed 9.8 million pounds. It had
to be moved to the launch pad. The Mobile

Service Structure had five movable platforms. It had two elevators. It was brought to the launch pad on the Transporter. It was a kind of towering "workroom." Here engineers, scientists, and other workers took care of all the last-minute details before launch. When everything was finally in order, the structure was taken down. This was about 11 hours before blast-off. The Transporter took it back to its storage area.

Finally the *Saturn V* was ready for its journey. The <u>countdown</u> was moving down to T-zero. Then there was blast-off. Now it was the rocket's turn to serve as the mover. Its job was to move the *Apollo* space capsule away from Earth. Then it sent the capsule <u>hurtling</u> into space to the moon—some 238,000 miles away.

The great engines of the *Saturn V* <u>ignited</u> at T-zero. A great blast of fire and noise exploded from the base of the

rocket. Four support arms of the Mobile Launcher, however, still held the *Saturn V* in place. The engines generated a <u>thrust</u> of 7.5 million pounds. It took about six seconds. Then, the arms released the rocket. The *Saturn V* with its *Apollo* spacecraft and the mobile home for the three astronauts inside <u>surged</u> away from Earth.

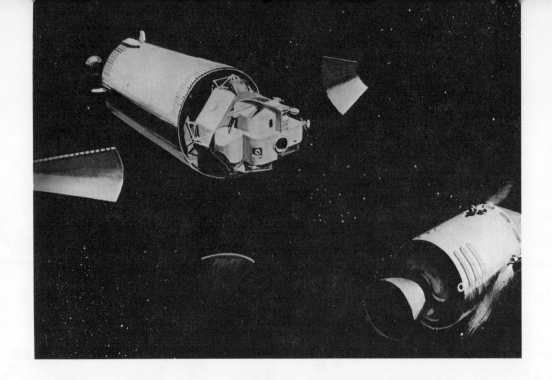

The three stages of the rocket dropped
off one by one as they completed their
individual tasks. *Apollo* continued on
through space to the moon. It went into
orbit around the moon. The Lunar
Landing Craft left it. It took two men down
to the surface of the moon. Then it
brought them back to the *Apollo*
spacecraft. The spacecraft returned to
Earth. A little more than eight days after
blast-off the astronauts were back home.
They had taken the longest round-trip
journey that any human being ever had.

GLOSSARY

Abandon / ə-'ban-dən: to leave

Aground / ə-'graund: to go onto the ground; with the bottom stuck on the ground

Allied / 'al-ˌīd: joined together to fight a common enemy

Antique / an-'tēk: not modern; belonging to the past

Asphalt / 'as-ˌfȯlt: a mixture of gravel and something like tar used to pave roads or streets

Assembled / ə-'sem-bəld: put together into a whole

Astronaut / 'as-trə-ˌnȯt: a pilot trained for space flight

Attached / ə-'tacht: connected or joined

Barge / 'bärj: a long, large boat with no power of its own used to move cargo

Berth / 'bərth: a place for a ship to be placed

Blast-off / 'blas-ˌtȯf: to take off into space; to launch a space vehicle

Cargo / 'kär-gō: freight carried by a ship, airplane, or other vehicle; a load

Channel / 'chan-əl: a trench through which water can flow

Code book / 'kōd 'bu̇k: a book that gives the answers to secret writing or signals

Compacted hydraulic fill / kəm-'pak-ted hī-'drȯ-lik 'fil: a material tightly packed together by the force of water put into a space

Compartment / kəm-'pärt-mənt: a part or a space into which a larger area is divided

Concrete cradle / 'kän-ˌkrēt 'krād-əl: a support to hold something, made of a hard substance that contains cement, sand, gravel, and water

Conning tower / 'kän-iŋ 'taủ(-ə)r: a raised structure on a submarine used for looking out

Construct / kən-'strəkt: to make or build

Core / 'kō(ə)r: the middle or center of anything

Countdown / 'kaủnt-ˌdaủn: to count backward to show the time needed to start an event; 3-2-1 go

Crane / 'krān: a machine used to lift or move heavy objects

Depth charge / 'depth 'chärj: an explosive weapon that is dropped into the water and used against submarines

Document / 'däk-yə-ˌment: a printed or written record used to prove something

Double-tracked crawler / 'dəb-əl-trakt 'krol-ər: a slow moving machine with two tanklike belts used to move large rockets

Duty / 'd(y)üt-ē: a tax paid on goods brought in from other countries

Engineer / ˌen-jə-'ni(ə)r: a person trained to work at planning and building roads, bridges, buildings, etc.

Epoxy resin / 'ep-ˌäk-sē 'rez-ᵊn: a material with a strong, hard, sticking quality

Excavator / 'ek-skə-ˌvāt-ər: a machine used to dig a hole or opening

Exhibit / ig-'zib-ət: to show or display to the public

Facing / 'fā-siŋ: the outer covering

Feat / 'fēt: something done that shows great courage or skill; a deed

Floating dry dock / 'flōt-iŋ drī däk: a structure that sits on water into which a boat can be put and lifted so it can be fixed

Foreign / 'fȯr-ən: from another country

Freighter / 'frāt-ər: a ship used for carrying cargo

Granite / 'gran-ət: a type of rock

Harbor /'här-bər: a place along the shore where a ship can come and anchor

Hitched / 'hicht: tied onto something; joined

Horsepower / 'hȯr-ˌspau̇(-ə)r: a measure of power equal to 550 foot-pounds per second

Hurtling / 'hərt-liŋ: moving quickly; rushing

Hydraulic excavator / hī-'drȯ-lik 'ek-skə-ˌvāt-ər: a machine that uses the force of water to dig holes

Ignited / ig-'nīt-ed: set on fire; lighted

Individual task / ˌin-də-'vij-(ə-)wəl 'task: a job done by one person or thing

Lacquer / 'lak-ər: a protective coating used to cover objects; similar to varnish

Land vehicle / 'land 'vē-ˌ(h)ik-əl: any means by which something is moved over the surface of the earth

Launch pad / 'lȯnch 'pad: a platform from which a rocket is put into space

Launched / 'lȯncht: floated a new ship into the water; sent off a rocket

Legal title / 'lē-gəl 'tīt-ᵊl: lawful right or claim

Maneuvers / mə-'n(y)ü-vər: movements or exercises

Masonry design / 'mās-ᵊn-rē di-'zīn: a stone or brick planned structure

Mechanical jack / **mi-**'kan-i-kəl 'jak: a device run by a machine used to raise objects

Median strip / 'mēd-ē-ən strip: a strip of land or pavement that divides the lanes of a highway

Memorial / mə-'mōr-ē-əl: something used to keep the memory of; remembrance

Mobile launcher / 'mō-bəl 'lȯn-chər: a moveable platform from which a rocket is lifted off

Periscope / 'per-ə-ˌskōp: a tube with mirrors used on a submarine so that the surface can be seen from under the water

Pier / 'pi(ə)r: a structure built out over the water and used as a landing place for boats

Platform / 'plat-ˌform: a flat surface higher than the ground or floor around it

Pneumatic breaker / n(y)u̇-'mat-ik 'brā-kər: a machine powered by air pressure used to separate hard materials

Preserved / pri-'zərvd: protected from damage; saved

Scientific / ˌsī-ən-'tif-ik: having to do with science

Scientists / 'sī-ənt-əsts: persons who study things in science

Scrapped / 'skrapt: gotten rid of

Secrecy / 'sē-krə-sē: keeping secret or hidden

Sonar / 'sō-ˌnär: a device used to locate objects under water by sending out sound waves that strike an object and bounce back

Space capsule / 'spās 'kap-səl: the part of a spaceship where the astronauts are

Spacecraft / 'spā-ˌskraft: a vehicle used in outer space

Submarine / 'səb-mə-ˌrēn: a kind of ship that can travel under the surface of the water

Support beam / sə-'po(ə)rt 'bēm: a post used to hold something up

Surfaced / 'sər-fəst: came to the top of the water

Surge / 'sərj: a sudden, strong rush

T-zero / 'tē-'zē-(ˌ)rō: the moment when a spacecraft is launched; when time has run out

Tanker / 'taŋ-kər: a vehicle used to move oil or other liquids

Thrust / 'thrəst: the forward force made by an engine

Torpedo / tȯr-'pēd-(ˌ)ō: a large explosive fired from a submarine to blow up other ships

Torpedo tube / tȯr-'ped-(ˌ)ō 't(y)üb: the place in a submarine from which a torpedo is launched

Tow line / 'tō 'līn: a rope or chain used to pull something

Winch / winch: a machine with a drum that turns, used for pulling

Wolf pack / 'wu̇lf 'pak: a group of submarines that stay together to hunt other ships and sink them

Zero in / 'zē-(ˌ)rō 'in: to focus on; to fix attention on

INDEX

ABOUT THE AUTHOR

David Paige is a former editor-in-chief for a book publisher who specialized in children's books. For the past seven years, he has devoted his time to fulltime writing. He lives in a suburb of Chicago with his wife and three children.